SWEET REPETITION

PHOENIX POETS
Edited by Srikanth Reddy
Rosa Alcalá, Douglas Kearney &
Katie Peterson, consulting editors

Sweet Repetition

CYNTHIA CRUZ

THE UNIVERSITY OF CHICAGO PRESS
CHICAGO & LONDON

The University of Chicago Press, Chicago 60637
The University of Chicago Press, Ltd., London

For more information, contact the University of Chicago Press, 1427 E. 60th St., Chicago, IL 60637.
Published 2025
Printed in the United States of America

34 33 32 31 30 29 28 27 26 25   1 2 3 4 5

ISBN-13: 978-0-226-84376-6 (paper)
ISBN-13: 978-0-226-84377-3 (ebook)
DOI: https://doi.org/10.7208/chicago/9780226843773.001.0001

Library of Congress Cataloging-in-Publication Data

Names: Cruz, Cynthia, author.
Title: Sweet repetition / Cynthia Cruz.
Other titles: Phoenix poets.
Description: Chicago : The University of Chicago Press, 2025. | Series: Phoenix poets | Includes bibliographical references.
Identifiers: LCCN 2025008159 | ISBN 9780226843766 (paperback) | ISBN 9780226843773 (ebook)
Subjects: LCGFT: Poetry.
Classification: LCC PS3603.R893 S94 2025 | DDC 811/.6—dc23/eng/20250328
LC record available at https://lccn.loc.gov/2025008159

♾ This paper meets the requirements of ANSI/NISO Z39.48-1992 (Permanence of Paper).

You speak of habit
as if things do not change I speak
of sweet repetition.

LIAM RECTOR, "Driving November"

CONTENTS

SWEET REPETITION

ONE

Nachtstilleben

What is memory
Undone by wonder.

Majesty, mystery,
Wonder, wonder.

Tripping through the exits
Of night, one dream

Foretells another
Drowning. One dream says,

I won't be alone.
Another says,

Childhood. Tarot and smoke,
Burn holes and handfuls

Of penny candy.
The boys are beautiful.

Tricked out in silver
Tinsel and snow paste,

Done up in blue
And dreamfuls

Of soft white powder.
Moving through the trance-

Like cemeteries
Of history

As in a dream.
Or, How do we exit.

The television static has been playing
The same Maria Callas

Song for days, for centuries.
If Mother didn't love me,

She wouldn't have told me
How to enter into the ocean

And vanish into the pinhole
Of my mind's blue

Night. Night's blue
Night—

Lamb

After Marni Ludwig

Always, there is the wish to vanish.
And the problem of not enough.

Then, death as the means of reversal.
Sorrow can't be located,

Only traced to a childhood
Gesture enacting the night

Of the world. I told you
Loss can draw a secret

To its birth. But I was blonde
And I was lying.

After Platonov

Over the earth,
A white bell in the sky,
Radiating, like madness.
By eleven, there were already
Yellow horses and something
Wondrous
Singing in the miracle
Of its sleep.
Her face, an ictus of stars.
Before the first morning,
I had already invented
A new instrument of religion,
Constructed of glue, gauze,
And the whinny of an old black horse.
In the dream, the wolf appears to me.
I do not know its name.
But in the chemical
Yellow of the forest,
I studied the aura of its paw,
The soundlessness of its memory.
Even as a child,
Already, it was too late.

Clinic

The star, reversed,
Means no hope.

All promise offered
Can only be false.

The answer to the question,
A shining list of symptoms.

A tremendous red ribbon
Coming down from the sun.

This ecstatic suspension
Between two worlds.

Self-Portrait in Parked Red Camaro, Modesto, California

Nutella smeared on cardboard.
Darth Vader

Child-sized t-shirt.
Silver, metal desert.

White diaphanous pearls
Of white sugar

Mixed with warm water
And powders of milk.

Telepathy, a starlike
Pattern of questions

In German, unanswerable,
Sequestered at the edge.

A man, his face
Coated in the soft warm

White of child's cream.
A cane in his hand and an animal

Coming out
From the meow of the dream.

Saint Paul, alone
Along the road,

Walking silently
Into his becoming.

Sleep as act
Or ritual

In preparation
For death.

What is the question,
She asks.

There is darkness. Then
There is another,

Further
Darkness.

A child's woolen blanket
Covers me.

Cream and fawn
Plush animals

Held together
With glossy ribbon.

What, she asks,
Is the question.

Fragment (Dora)

Dora on her back
On the soft leather couch,
Dreaming annihilation.

Circuitous, the drive
And its liquid, libidinous loop

Looping back endlessly
To its ruinous and glorious
Origin.

After Platonov

Over the earth, the nadir of death.
By evening there were ribbons and singing.
The child is not dead. She is sleeping
Among the other sleeping children.
Her face, a condensation of stars,
And sorrow. Already, I have invented an apparatus
For dreaming, constructed of memory,
Pale-pink cream frosting, and the whinny
Of a small white horse. In the dream, the future
Appears to me. History's dissolution, retroactively
Traced back. Inside the mirage of night, I reappear.
Then vanish. Even as a child, I already belonged
To death. A symptom, I am the answer
To my own hopeless question.

Clinic

Whose horses.
And ruinous,

The way she leads them
Back into the skein
Of its dream

From the semblance
From which it derives
Its blonde never.

It wants to return, to hide back
Inside the small silk canister
That the mind makes
Of the detritus, the excrement

Of memory,
That stays behind
Inside the mind's blue night.

This world in which
There is no world.

Raspberry Syrup

Pet,
we're all of us a little bit horses
each of us in his own way's a horse.

VLADIMIR MAYAKOVSKY

In winter, walking to Schönbrunn
With Mother in the snow,
I saw a white horse
Falling down into the street,
Its legs kicking wildly.

I became the white horse,
Neighing into the cold void
Of that black Viennese night.

Horses that fall; spotted horses
Attached to carts; black horses;
White horses; small horses that whinny;
Horses that don't; horses, their lithe bodies
Linked to carriages, chained to posts;
Horses that can't be trained, that cannot
Be tamed. I want to be

Devoured
By horses,

To enter the impossible
Kingdom of their secret
Animal silence.

Because of the horses
Because of the horses

The children I am friends with
In the childhood dream
Keep singing to me.
Sister, Mother, birth and death,
Mother, Father, Hanna.

I want to have my own
Children. I play master
With the papier-mâché mansion
I made of paper
That I turn into
An orphanage.
I turn into
A pale plaster and paper
Embryo opera house.

All the singing
Of the orphans
Inside the membrane
Of the paper house.

Always a premonition
Of danger. Of fire and
Of falling white and black horses.

I say, Enter the horses.
I enter the horses.

Infinite, the movement
Of always leaving and returning.
Always leaving and returning.

And the now-mother
Hanna and the spectacle
Of not merely the rejection
But of her having been

Stricken and made
Invisible.

I take the cake filled with Chantilly
Cream and wild raspberries, covered with pink
Almond paste and royal icing
From out of the *Kühlschrank*.
I cut into the rose-colored sponge cake
With the sharp silver knife.

When I take the paper giraffe
Away from the paper giraffe,
It makes its terrible crying

Stop. Horses drawing
A cart that carries
The embellished black-and-white
Coffin with a hidden
Body within it.
Then the black and white horses
Awaken from the dream.
And they begin
Their relentless and miraculous racing.

A Horse Striking Its Hoof on the Ground at Midnight

Now, a child's glittering black horse,
Swimming.

When it stops,
I stop breathing.

I am still waiting
For the right words

To begin
Speaking.

Or is this what it means
Not to be human.

I drank the small substance
Until I dropped
Into a shallow sleep-

Less dream. The soldiers
Were not unkind, their bodies

Concealed inside the shadows
Of history.

History, concealed
Within its own
Shadow.

This moment
Is neither now

Nor in the future.
It is both but also

Something else
Entirely.

Repetition repeats
But also secretes
Something within it,

A substance,
The end

Of all things.
But also

The beginning
Of something

Entirely
Without precedent.

After Platonov

Over the earth, already, the zero hour.
By eleven, already, the unimaginable
And its delicate murmur
Of liquid magnetics. The sleeping
Child is not sleeping. She is
Dreaming among the dreaming
Children. Her face, a mask,
An empty trembling.
A proliferating contagion
Among the otherworldly
Flowers. Already I have invented
A new form of religion. Part female,
Part animal, constructed of crimson
Duct tape, cardboard, and the miraculous
Whinny of a galloping white horse.
In the dream, the Holy Spirit
Appears to me, disguised
As an orphaned child.
At night I sleep in the garden,
Waiting for the undead to begin
Their miraculous singing.

Play in Which Darkness Falls

Fear of horses transforms
Into a compulsion
To look at horses.

I have to look at horses, then
I become frightened again.

Mother tells me
Not to look at them.

In the dream, I take the giraffe
From the giraffe. It is
Taken away. *Weg-*
Genommen.

I take the animal,
And I crumple it.

What, father asks.
I say, A gun for shooting.

I say, A horse
Falling in the street.

A horse, falling
In the street.

It died. No, it
Didn't die.

It runs through the dead
City at night.

In the dream, Mother
Is gone, and I have no one
To *schmiege* with.

No one to snuggle with,
To double with.

A horse from my dreams
Will walk in from the Viennese
City street and enter the bedroom.

I put my hand
Over the horse's O
Of its open mouth.

Don't put your hand
Over the mouth
Of the horse's
Mouth.

My little sister is
The little giraffe.
The papier-mâché
Giraffe.

In the glacial night
Of her far-off dreams,
My sister says to me,

There is no safety
In removing oneself

From the scene.

TWO

In This Light the Junk Undergoes a Transfiguration; It Shines

In the interview recorded the night before
His final death, he said he was almost nearly

Adjacent to being human.
In the basement apartment,

My mother tells me
On the long-distance telephone

My body is slowly
Filling with light.

I don't believe I have ever
Told you that I never

Look at my own face
In the mirror.

The rain outside is starling.
It is the color of the silver

Fur of the animal the woman wears
In the story where she becomes

The animal. Last night's dream
Is entering my body again,

Like the dream
Between the end and the beginning

Of history, which has yet
To begin. The world, still in its prehistoric

Silver-dawn atmosphere.
In the broken glass of the last

Atmosphere, someone finally
Calls out my name. I am

Finally becoming
What I was meant

To become,
Disintegrating what's left
Of the blonde girl I thought
I was. In the clinic,

Deniz is becoming
Thin from the leukemia. *Hello,*

He says, *Hello*.
The last time I saw him,

His delicate and otherworldly
Black-and-white drawings

Of houses on fire,
Taped with Scotch tape

To the walls
Of his locked bedroom.

Wandering the long, locked halls,
A child, locked inside the body

Of a man locked inside the body
Of a beautiful and lonely child.

Nachtstilleben

Come with me
If there is a world.

Animal, mineral,
Sticky star

Formed of silver,
Crystal globs

In the form of stars.
In the form

Of mother love.
Junk summer

Whistling its memory back
Into me.

Cindy and the jets.
Cindy and the silver

Window at the edge
Of the world. Cindy

Invisibilizing herself
Back into that black winter.

Star ride, star ride.
The world isn't so bad.

Come let me
Hold your hand.

You never
Have to be

In this world this
Alone again.

Untitled

Death on the line,
Murmuring its obscene
Numbers.

We never had any money,
Always selling something

To eat something
Or another. Ho Hos or cola.
Cold coffee and American cigarettes.

Sitting outside the food store,
Counting numbers: dollars,
Pennies, nickels, quarters.

Money whispers.
It has nothing

But death
On its mind.

Charity Balls

After John Wieners

I had an accident but lived in elegance
On methamphetamines, and small stacks
Of *Black Beauty* paperbacks,
Plastic plates of bread,
And black cherry marmalade.
Later, a career of killing time
And wasting money.
But I have always been extraordinarily gifted
At being alone. At the age of five,
I thought I would never speak.
It wasn't until I was thirteen
That I knew it to be true.
In blonde wig, old worn denim, and gold
Chain with plastic pink Saint Genet pendant,
I enter the terminal infirmary of music
And move the body as though
Engaged in infinite reenactments
Of the sacred. Murmuring among my people
In the ruins of the institutions of this city.
Awaiting dispersal of food stamps and low-cost medicines.
But I always knew if I worked hard enough,
I would never make it.

Fragment

The star in the animal's heart
Makes the animal cry.

It is the loneliness
Of the annihilation

Of all the others
Who have gone before it.

It knows its end
Is coming.

And with it, the vanishing
Of the world.

It sleeps beneath the tree
As the shadow

Begins.

Charity Balls

After John Wieners

I had an accident but lived in opulence
And poverty, lacking nothing. One night
As a gesture, I stole my brother's black penknife,
Cut all my long blonde hair off. Joan of Arc,
Racing through the French fifteenth century
On the back of her mad horse.
I sustained myself on its probability
And handfuls of night
Capsules. Later, a career of trying
To enter the question. *Lean closer,*
She whispers, both of us gathered on the gold-
Flecked tile of my childhood bathroom.
At the age of five, I thought I had died.
It wasn't until I turned
Twenty-two that I knew it to be true.
Lemon buttercream triple-layered
Wedding cake and chocolate
Chiffon scarf thrown over the bedside
Porcelain. I started speaking of
My desire and the radiant suspension
Between being and becoming. I am
Pathologically shy, infantile, and obsessive
By nature. But I always knew
If I worked hard enough,
Even then, I would never
Make it.

California

Back home
In California,

In my home
Where I am

Not. The milk
And stars stuck

In the black crown.
And the swarming

Crowds, moving
Like mercury, adjusting

To the new order. A hover
Of blinding-white bees

Transforming according
To velocity.

I am not afraid. I am
Not the animal

That is
Not the animal.

Each of us, she says,
Is alone.

Each of us
Praying along the glittering

Edge.

Nachtstilleben

White on white galloping horseback.
Yellow and its yellow blare of radio sun
Over the hillside, on the yellow
Corner of blood-soaked page.
Quiet and its quieted child.
Its animal voice.
Its natural and inevitable arrival.
Death and its high priestess, her magnificent
Crown, its red globs, its paper cutout
Angels, its sickly strings.
Black stuck deep in its maddening black haloing crown.
What is the title of the book she is holding.
Death spilling out from its pages.
Her blue columns of night.
And already, the expanding pools.
The sick children, waiting.
The angel, his elbow covered in cigarette ash.
And judgment, the pretty blonde
Angel, its yellow metal flute,
A red carnation in its hair,
Blood on the sheen of its wing.

White Porcelain

The yellow sun appears
Suddenly, a direct, collect call

From a desert motel room
A lifetime of cities away.

Outside, near the ruins
Of the abandoned power station,

Four white wolves
Dream, sleeping in the warm

White foam
Of their one shared dream.

Charity Balls

After John Wieners

I had an accident but lived in decadence
On stolen boxes of Swiss chocolate,
Pasolini poems, and cards of the lives of the saints.
Later, a career of sleeping on the porcelain floors
Of hotel bathrooms, warm milk in white tubs and sinks.
But beneath the symptoms, and mountains
Of meticulously calculated plans, I have always been a child.
At the age of twenty-nine, I desired
To become a writer. It was not until the age of thirty-seven
That I knew it would never come true.
Lottery tickets and plastic bags of glass
Bottles, barefoot in a cream-white
Evening gown and silver halo
Of paper cutout stars, I began speaking
In a language I could no longer comprehend.
I am self-destructive by nature, my body
Submerged in the animal silence
Of shame. But I knew
If I gave away everything I would never have,
Only then would I become human.

Day One

Black ponies, glass windows, yellowing
Hillsides, detective novels. Girls in cream-
White face paint, hiding inside the world
Outside the world. I slept with my black
Bear and never spoke, or only in gesture:
My small hand drawing a small world
On bits of scrap paper. Wild foxes,
Their warm bodies merged in mange,
Desire, and deathly illness, creeping
Through the blinding wet gauze of daylight.
When I stroke the animal's warm white neck,
It purrs, like an animal. I perform death,
Its final three stages, and trace the language
Of its incision, listening for its godlike ring.

This Accident That Was My Life

After Denis Johnson After Vladimir Mayakovsky

It's after one. You're probably no longer
Alive. All night the night rings like a sun
In the tollbooth of our foreverness. Now is the hour
One is undone. Hello, my darling, my king, my delicate
Animal. I am undone. Like a dream undone
From a gold jewel box, spilling with wet
White pearls of animal tenderness, this dream
That was my life will have its witnesses,
While the ocean lies in its tremendous
Blue bed and sorry in its turbulence
Of stars. Now is the hour
One speaks to the patterns of unrevolving
History and the universe. I swear
You will never hear my voice again.

Nachtstilleben

White on white galloping horseback.
Black in its black arrow and
Death in its disintegrating
Blue and red radio blare
Of disintegrating red
Orb of the sun. Silence
And its silent child. Its fluttering flag
Of warm white petrol. Death, abstracted
And detached. Let loose and dissolved
Into all things animate and inanimate.
Death with its empty black *Punkt*.
Its pearled crown of wet
White children's glue.
Its holes of death
Stuck in every black,
In every hovering
Blue aura
Of sniper-blue
Night.

Charity Balls

After John Wieners

I had a fellowship but lived poorly
On cheap beer and penny candy.
Later, a career of killing time,
But I have always been
Ashamed of what I am.
At the age of five, I thought I would never
Amount to anything. It was not until I turned
Thirty-eight that I knew it would be true.
Moving like a shadow through the rooms
Of this century, chalk-blue
Carnations in my long, blonde hair.
I'm obsessive by nature,
Hysterical, infantile, and often, a liar.
But I always knew, were I born
Again, even then,
I would never survive.

Clinic

The letters and poems you wrote
Are lucid and anything
But evidence of madness.
If by madness
What we mean
Is a lack of meaning.
Your poems and your letters
Are your attempt at saying
What cannot be said
In language. To touch
The impossible,
What lies beyond
The cut of language.

The wild foxes
Along the border
Of the clinic,
No one else
Can see them.
Hungering, as they are
At the edge of everything
That is beyond meaning.

Day One

Yellow hooves, car lots, Star Wars
T-shirt, and skateboards. *King Lear*
And *Hamlet*. My father's being
Made his becoming
American impossible. I was always
Ahead, but I never experienced
Any of it. An animal.
If I would, I would be
A white rabbit. A white, long-haired rabbit.
Or white horses, swimming
Beneath. What I remember
Is everything. And what I don't
Are the endless processions
Of animals—foxes, horses,
And the black *x*'s of black
Bats soaring above.
The silent masked and haloed
Children making their way
Through the small Mexican village.

Untitled

Songbird
In the city garden
Sounding at night.

Singing something

No one understands
But nonetheless
Hums along:

Because the world is gone.
The world is gone.

THREE

All of Us or None

After Brecht

And we made a tunnel
Through the darkening

Tunnel. You, me,
And all the others.

The blackening
Gelatinous junk

Funneling something
That is nothing,

Coating
Everything.

Nothing left
But this invisible,

Supreme static
Radio coming in

Through the breaking
Rooms of glass

Windows. F-16s
In the English language

Dropping smoldering
Leaflets, warning

Of the coming—
We were

Hungering
For something,

Reduced
To nothing.

Mere animal.
Crawling

In the interstice,
In the in-between

Interstice between
Worlds.

Swimming
In the warning

Of what was once
America.

I was so filled up
With its excess, its

Nothingness.
There was nothing.

Transposed, then
Transformed into quickening

Melody, something
Repetitive and speculative

Like this: We were
So filled up with the nothing.

There was nothing
But leaving

Left. Moving from
One city to another,

Moving through
One world

Into another. One
Of us,

All of us,
And always

More of us.
It is only those

Who have nothing
Who can save

Those who have
Nothing.

Everything or nothing,
All of us or none.

We were poor when we were
Born, and we'll be born

Again when we're
Transformed

As the next
Form. Human

Desire for nothing.
Human drive

To follow that desire,
Tethered to nothing.

Only tethered to
One another.

And as we die
Through the darkness,

Moving our bodies
Through the blinding

Tunnels under what's left
Of what was America—

You, me,
And all the others.

Everything
Or nothing.

All of us
Or none.

ACKNOWLEDGMENTS

I would like to thank the editors of the following publications, in which versions of some of these poems first appeared:

Alta Journal: “Self-Portrait in Parked Red Camaro, Modesto, California”
Berlin Lit: “Clinic” (“Whose horses”), both poems titled “Day One,” “Fragment,” and “A Horse Striking Its Hoof on the Ground at Midnight” (as “Clinic”)
Copper Nickel: “Fragment (Dora)”
The Kenyon Review: “California”
Nimrod: “This Accident That Was My Life”
The New Republic: “Clinic” (“The letters and poems you wrote”)
The Paris Review: “Charity Balls” (“I had an accident but lived in elegance”)
Poem-a-Day (Academy of American Poets): “In This Light the Junk Undergoes a Transfiguration; It Shines”
The Queens Review: “White Porcelain” (as “My California”)

NOTES ON THE TEXT

This collection's epigraph is taken from Liam Rector's poem "Driving November," in *The Sorrow of Architecture* (Dragon Gate Press, 1984).

The title "Nachtstilleben" is from Wolfgang Tillmans's photograph *Nachtstilleben (Night Still Life)*, 2011 (negative), 2013 (print).

"Lamb" is informed by and structured after Marni Ludwig's poem "Lamb," in *Pinwheel* (New Issues Poetry and Prose, 2013).

The beginning of the first lines of the poems titled "After Platonov"—"Over the earth"—originates from Andrei Platonov's novel *The Foundation Pit*.

"Fragment (Dora)" refers to Freud's unfinished psychoanalytic case study, *Fragment of an Analysis of a Case of Hysteria*.

The poems "Raspberry Syrup," "A Horse Striking Its Hoof on the Ground at Midnight," and "Play in Which Darkness Falls" are in conversation with Freud's psychoanalytic case study of Little Hans and, more specifically, Darian Leader's essay "Rereading Little Hans" (supplement, *Journal of the Centre for Freudian Analysis and Research* [July 2021]).

The epigraph to "Raspberry Syrup" is from "Kindness to Horses," in *Vladimir Mayakovsky: Poems*, translated by Dorian Rottenberg (Progress Publishers, 1972).

"Play in Which Darkness Falls" is the title of a Frank Stanford poem in the unpublished collection "Automatic Co-Pilot."

"In This Light the Junk Undergoes a Transfiguration; It Shines" comes from the Bible.

The poems in the "Charity Balls" series are informed by and structured after John Wieners's poem "Charity Balls," in *Supplication: Selected Poems of John Wieners*, edited by Joshua Beckman, CAConrad, and Robert Dewhurst (Wave Books, 2015).

"This Accident That Was My Life" is informed by and structured after Denis Johnson's poem "After Mayakovsky," which is informed by and structured after the fragment of a poem in Vladimir Mayakovsky's suicide note.

The final poem of this collection, "All of Us or None," is informed by Bertolt Brecht's poem of the same title.